POSITIVE TIPS

FOR

STRESS

(ENGLISH EDITION)

VIJAYKUMAR GUMMADI

NOTION PRESS

NOTION PRESS

India. Singapore. Malaysia.

Published by Notion Press 2023

Copy Right© VijayKumar Gummadi 2023
All rights reserved

ISBN 979-888951963-8

Dedicated

to

my daughter

Gummadi Pavani

Foreword

Stress is part of modern lifestyle. No one is immune to stress. Everyday every one experiences some sort of stress or other.

Using medicines last resort to manage stress if you can't manage with other positive methods.

We cannot do anything other than managing stress in modern life.

This book 'POSITIVE TIPS FOR STRESS' brings out 501 nos life changing tips for managing and coping with stress.

Definitely this book tips will reduce your stress levels drastically.

This book is highly useful and must read for all especially to women and students.

♣♠♣

♣♣♣(1)♣♣♣

Everyone wants to be healthy, happy and rich without paying price. The price is effort. You know very well what you need to do to achieve your objectives. But you want to follow fastest and easy path of shortcuts by following least resistant path. For wants and needs your objective is same. The risk difference in between paths of wants and needs give rise to stress. Hence always follow right path with genuine efforts to achieve your goals in personal and professional lives.

♣♣♣(2)♣♣♣

There is nothing in this world that you can't learn. Only difference between people is time taken for learning. As an individual you have limited time. You need knowledge and expertise in many areas as you set sail through your personal and professional lives. But you can't learn all for yourself during your finite life. No one can possibly know everything. But your intention to learn everything for yourself creates unnecessary stress for you as you can never achieve objectives. Hence where ever and whenever required seek out help of experts and specialists in personal and professional lives. You should always seek practical knowledge from a perfect source. You need no reason to help people. Help is done by heart not by mind.

♣♣♣(3)♣♣♣

Lack of self discipline is root cause to most of the failures giving raise to anxiety and stress. Even an average person can be successful with self discipline. Even blessing background, good education and experience can't help without self discipline. You need not be extraordinary to be successful. Discipline is the link between your goals and accomplishments.

♣♣♣(4)♣♣♣

People put less energy in achieving their goals and more energy in making up excuses creating unnecessary stress.

When you put effort to make progress rather making excuses it sets you free from stress. Excuses continue to make excuses, excuses have cascading cycle. People with enormous self-control can only refuse to make excuses. Repeated justifications or excuses are never beneficial to yourself, they provide easy escape from real required change. Excuses or justifications will drive you away from uncomfortable feelings of facing reality.

♣♣♣(5)♣♣♣

As long as your actions, what ever you say and do are consistent with your long term goals and objectives you are normal and free from stress. Long-term thinking makes one successful. The difference between short-term and long-term perspective is a cause of anxiety and stress. Temporary fix always boomerangs.

♣♣♣(6)♣♣♣

When you live in complete truth with yourself you are true to your personal and professional lives. Self denial of this truth gives directly or indirectly stress. Truthfulness guarantees all other values. When you are true to self you will good about yourself. Inner realization is far more reliable than any other knowledge. We feel denial of truthfulness is the ultimate comfort zone for us. Truth prevails only when all similar persons are treated equal. Truth can't exist where ignorance is practiced. Your world is your reality. Always find true reason.

In a modern world of illusions it is very difficult to find the truth. Most of the facts are exaggerated and presented. Reality looks wrong but dreams look real. Stress is generated when you don't live in reality. No body is 100% truthful or transparent. People do have their own secret agenda.

♣♣♣(7)♣♣♣

Decisions are unavoidable. Decision making is always stressful due to uncertainties involved. Your decisions show your values and priorities.

Self reflection enables to choose among alternatives and temptations in decision making. Never make permanent decisions on temporary feelings. We pretend to remain blind and don't want to see what exists in our inner self.

♣♣♣(8)♣♣♣

Fundamental cause for stress in your life is you will feel someone else is responsible for your life. You always crave for others approval and do things as others wanted. You never wanted to do things as you wish and let others hijack your life. When something goes wrong in your life you blame others. You never realize that others are never under your control. Everything happens to you the main thing is what how you respond to what happens to you. People never realize the fact that they have to endure consequences of situations out of their control. Freedom is responsibility. It is great to be responsible. Only few abide by their responsibility.

♣♣♣(9)♣♣♣

When we are negative, we doubt and see worst in others undermining their good intended actions. Negativity blinds us and prevents us from seeking and seeing the truth.

♣♣♣(10)♣♣♣

Money is the biggest problem and concern in life. Most of negative emotions directly or indirectly associated with money. You are directly responsible for your financial life and you can never blame others for this. Truthfully accept responsibility for your income, expenditure and investments. Punish financial misbehavior. Seek accountability of financial responsibilities. Carryout regular financial audits to improve financial system. Make provisions for unexpected uncertainties. Money kills most of the human problems of modern world. You can be richer by limiting your desires. Money can change attitudes of people you never expected. Wealth generates envy. Money induces selfishness and irresistibly invites abuse.
Right place to store Money is head not in heart.

Just control your money it controls your everything. If you lose money, money starts controlling you. Not earning but managing money is real problem for Wealth creation in the modern world due to too many distractions.

♣♣♣(11)♣♣♣

Sense of control is important in life. Unchecked freedom derails your life, anything too much is too bad, some restraint is always required to have balance in life. Don't allow selfish people control your life who did little to your life. Your personality is beautiful when your attitude is under control. When nothing is under control just relax don't get stressed for no reason. When control is lost at least try to control affect of consequences. Either you control your life or remain as one controlled in life. People resist unknown due to fear of loss of control. Self control is most important before you do anything.

♣♣♣(12)♣♣♣

95% of people don't have goals and plans for their objectives. Simply they don't know what to do now and then. If you work on a goal everyday goal moves towards you. Unless whole team wins goal, no one wins. Individual achievements are fine for historical records. Unrealistic and unclear goals cause confusion and distress. Be realistic, don't waste time trying impossible targets. Goal is automatic order against laziness. You can't achieve your goal because you are not attached to your goal but to your personality. Goal is measured by outcomes not by intentions. Stress is generated when you are not in a position to choose out of simultaneously two wanting goals. One will also become stressful due to conflict in desires vs pains in gaining them.

♣♣♣(13)♣♣♣

Life is full of problems to be resolved. Instead of blaming others adopt a solution for what can be done now. Problems remain unresolved when we failed to apply our knowledge. If we continue our journey down the wrong road it give enormous distress.

Spend less time on diagnosis more time for finding solutions. You can never solve problems on your own. Many problems are created by our imagination. Distinguish between work related problems and personal problems. Act promptly on genuine problems. Most of the times we don't want to give either answer or true solution but just we want to manage show by just coping. If you want to address a problem, problem must be defined in a straightforward manner but not like beating around bush. This is a first step towards real transformation. The problem is not what your circumstances are but rather how you are.Root to fundamental problem is disorganization. Most of our decisions are based fear of how others view & feel us rather on truth. Our subconscious mind is auto protective, always focuses and spends time on convincing people who don't like us rather with people who love and care us. This is the reason why we spend more time on problems than on solutions. We try to address and fix symptoms not problems. We talk about selective problems and stay quite about other problems.

♣♣♣(14)♣♣♣

Happiness and distress depends on state of mind. Disease begins in mind with poisonous thoughts. Cultivate cheerfulness even in odd circumstances. Our body automatically reacts to every thought we have. For proper functioning of mind you should know how to harness the power of intellect. What exhaust your mind controls your life.

♣♣♣(15)♣♣♣

If you harbor attachment, detachment causes stress. See things as they are without attachment. Attachment creates desire. Attachment makes one intentionally and unintentionally biased and erroneous. We are extremely sensitive to rejection.

♣♣♣(16)♣♣♣

Any thing unused will automatically decay like rusting.

When unused you are likely to forget knowledge when you most need. Forgetfulness and timely your inability to recall knowledge will adversely affects intellect of your mind. Knowledge in order to be promptly applied it must always remain with you. Hence knowledge internal revision is essential and necessary to maintain level of your intellect.

♣♣♣(17)♣♣♣

World is full of innumerable unwanted stimuli. Don't be drifted away by distractions which cause distress. Walk by faith in your goal not by sight. There may be thousands of things that can irritate, worry or distract you. Don't let small things bother you just ignore them.

♣♣♣(18)♣♣♣

You can't eliminate stressful situations. However all you have to do is respond to these situations without generating emotional stress. Unaddressed emotions can seed stress and unhappiness. Your emotions are you, reflection of you. Main reason for most of human actions is emotion. You can quench others emotions just by making them to understand. Emotional oscillations ultimately drive behavior to reach psychological equilibrium tranquility.

♣♣♣(19)♣♣♣

Time spent on our priorities is more important than total hours spent. When you can't control your time you can't control your life. Eliminate activities that are waste of time or gives endless distractions. You care time time cares your everything else. Your time shows what is really matters in your life. Uncontrollable time forces you to accept circumstances. Stress is inversely proportional to time available. Time is most common root cause of stress.

♣♣♣(20)♣♣♣

Whatever stress management technique you adopt is ineffective unless you know origin of stress. If you want to be free from stress you should get rid of root cause.

We feel stressed when we are attached ourselves to consequence of particular outcome and we are not in a position to accept possible results. When you focus on efforts not on results you will not be stressed.

♣♣♣*(21)*♣♣♣

Adopting to better style of working eliminates stress. Perform your individual duties along with your team for achieving objectives.

Work load never breaks you down, but the way you do things.

♣♣♣*(22)*♣♣♣

Change can't happen overnight or instantly. Change is stressful until you acclimate to new environment or conditions. You have to carryout sustainable changes bit by bit even if they are discomfortable. Change must be based on strengths. Your resistance for change automatically dissolves when expected change is safe. Resistance coexists with a reason. You can change only when you detach your self from your past and attach to your future.

♣♣♣*(23)*♣♣♣

Your imagination and visualization can never compensate for work undone. Lies cannot be visualized. Think about the task in front of you and put relentless effort. Memory and intellect both are essential for productivity. No one can do what you can only do. Your productive time should be focused on true priorities. Focus on tasks not on individuals. True feedback is a reflection of sincerity. You can't be productive when your personality and environment are unsynchronized and misaligned. Most of the times we are non productive due to our irrational fear of illusionary worst happening.

♣♣♣*(24)*♣♣♣

However busy you may be you must make time to communicate. Communication is not feasible in a untrustful culture.

Problem with communication is we don't try to understand communication received rather we focus on giving reply for communication. Good communication is understanding misunderstanding.

♣♣♣(25)♣♣♣

Everyone does mistakes. Unadmitted mistakes are cause of distress. Admit your mistakes before anyone else has a chance to point them out. You are responsible and accountable for your own mistakes.

♣♣♣(26)♣♣♣

Taming your worries is important. You always need some quite time break for regeneration. No outward accomplishment can give your prolonged tranquility. We crave for self isolation when there is mismatch between who we want to be and who actually we are.

♣♣♣(27)♣♣♣

Most people won't give honest feedback due to selfishness or fear. Honesty is first chapter for book of education.
Just by creating rules can't make people honest. Honestly is expensive, hence few allow to practice it.
We lie to ourselves we project ourselves OK in front of others though not.
You prevent help being coming to you, as you are not honest to yourself ,you never intend to be true to yourselves.

♣♣♣(28)♣♣♣

You have to invest significant time, money and energy in continuously developing self w.r.t. time. Otherwise technological innovations and inventions as well as obsolescence are occurring at rapid phase that can make your stressful in adopting to new changes.

♣♣♣(29)♣♣♣

Conflicts are common, unavoidable and not preventable. Conflict is not good versus bad, but it is one man's belief versus another man's belief. Real conflict is in between your heart and mind. Honest conversations could fix many conflicts.

When your heart wins over your mind you won the conflict. Biased solutions for conflicts drifts your plan from main course permanently. Conflicts are built up dye to avoidance and autocratic thinking.

♣♣♣(30)♣♣♣

Your relationships will be good as along as you control your emotions. People could never control their emotions fully. Your emotions are capable of over powering your emotions. Individuals are not capable of processing all types of emotions. Unprocessed emotions are root cause to behavior problems and symptoms. Most of the times we avoid to facing our own emotions due to fear of inability in handling them. You are automatically pulled towards fulfilling your emotional hunger and desires. You can live your life fully only when you are able to process all your emotions or else you are stuck. Best way of managing emotions is understanding them and experiencing them. However we do not want to face reality, we fear to face emotions. The problem surfaces when we don't make space for our emotions, when we avoid them. That results in odd emotional bursts affecting self and others as well as it causes frustration. Emotions are never true representation of our realities. While resorting to action based on emotions , you need to evaluate and filter emotions with rational logic. Unfulfilled emotional craving finds another way to satisfy its hunger. Many lack capability to process their feelings in real time.

♣♣♣(31)♣♣♣

You are prevented being optimistic when you are surrounded by pessimistic culture. When culture don't exists anarchy dominates.

♣♣♣(32)♣♣♣

Ego develops when you live in separation with others. Trust is inversely proportional to ego. Ego kills your relationships, your talents and your growth. Love and friendship can only melt Ego.

Egoist can sink a team. Your ego comes in the way to see things for what they are. We dislike and don't easily accept people more successful than us. We always try to find faults in their success.

♣♣♣(33)♣♣♣

Fear of unknown is main reason for procrastination. Being disorganized is main reason for procrastination. Your attachment to comfort makes you procrastinating. Procrastinating people replace accomplishments with Justifications and excuses.

♣♣♣(34)♣♣♣

Your suffering is proportional to your fear but not to the reality. Fear is more expensive than failure. We tend to lose lot of opportunities due to unexamined fears about our environment. Unaddressed irrational fears will become reality as they are preoccupied in your mind. We are aware what we want to do and what we need to do, but our actions are limited by our fears. Change or progress in life and work is only possible when our vision overcomes our fears. Never fight your fears rather go through them they dissolve. Your unvalidated imagination with logic makes things worse. Most of our feelings are reflection of our imagination rather reality. Your irrational fears are major contributors of your stress and anxiety. We are worried about unlikely and imaginary threat that we can't control. When you shield your mind it generates anxiety, panic and disturbance. If you act you don't fear.

♣♣♣(35)♣♣♣

Unchecked freedom can be expensive. Boundaries must be set for freedom. Freedom is granted to make you and others better. Freedom is not free. Freedom is your reaction to your circumstances.

♣♣♣(36)♣♣♣

Unchecked habit converts into necessity. The difference between good habit and bad habit is either you control the habit or habit controls you.

Bad habits resist change for good. Good habits are established gradually.

♣♣♣(37)♣♣♣

No one is really busy, it just your value in their priority list.
Never depend too much on any,
people do change with time and circumstances. Many give advice but few only really help.

♣♣♣(38)♣♣♣

What happens to your personal life is more important than what happening to professional life for deciding about your professional choices.

♣♣♣(39)♣♣♣

If you love others they are in your heart, if you hate others they are in your mind. Fact is humans can't be without humans. Relationships in life are supposed to enrich you. Your relationships must make sense to you but not to others. Not everyone deserves to know real you. True life is being real, humble, kind and loving. Life will become beautiful when you cease to be pessimistic. When you are joyful you perceive your world joyful. When you live life only to please others you are likely to become mad. You will feel fulfillment and satisfaction in life when you live by values you believe in. Have the courage to choose the life of your values. Living forward is what life actually is. Life without aim is lived with confusion. Small setbacks are part of life. Do things that will move life forward and progress. Only your rational mind has to guide you through your life but not your feelings. Joy is reality in life when you accommodate clarity, tranquility, purposefulness, healthfulness. Optimistic changes will occur in your life when live real life as who you are. Living true life is never to life as per expectations rather with uncertainty and randomness. Acceptance of others, their looks, their behaviors, their beliefs, bring you an inner peace and tranquility, instead of anger and resentment. Value of life is only known to those who has experienced adversity to adversity.

♣♣♣(40)♣♣♣

Love is a coin with two sides as pleasure and pain. Trust, loyalty and respect are more important in personal and professional lifes. Your absence wont teach them your value when your presence did not matter to them. Do not stay there where your presence being not appreciated. No matter how great you are, not everybody will like you, that is life. Learn to love yourself. You are amazing just the way you are. You deserve a relationship where you are celebrated instead tolerated. Love and ego can't reside in same room. Understanding is an art, not everyone is an artist. Love doesn't need to be perfect, love needs to be true. People are as beautiful as they love. Love makes you vulnerable. Your expression of fear or love indicates your deep personal attachment. It's a unconscious association. Love stops rationalized thinking and compels you to be vulnerable. It is easy to hate and it is difficult to love.

♣♣♣(41)♣♣♣

Mindfulness makes space, creates infinite capacity. When you live in present your understanding increases and thinking disappears. You can find solutions when you live in present. Mindfulness keeps you fit and healthy.

♣♣♣(42)♣♣♣

Don't take every issue too seriously. Maintain when you can't resolve. Addressing an issue is more important than winning an argument. Accept everyone has right to disagree. Acknowledge that there are upper and lower limitations everywhere. Everything has limits that make sense. Unmanaged emotions creates conflicts.

♣♣♣(43)♣♣♣

Life doesn't demand to be perfect, it seeks to be human. Be good don't be perfect. Consistency is critical than perfection. Once you accept your imperfections then only you can make things perfect. Absolute Perfectionism can ever be reached.

It is chasing a mirage. No one is perfect not even close to perfect. Perfectionism must take your capability into consideration. Instead of absolute Perfectionism, focus on progress with optimum Perfectionism.

♣♣♣(44)♣♣♣

Emotional self awareness is more important for a beautiful personality. Lack of empathy is due to lack of self awareness. Irrational people exhibit negativity.

♣♣♣(45)♣♣♣

How you behave is more important than what you know. Your environment decides your personality. Loss of self awareness often results in hijacking of personality due to irreversible sabotage done by our irrational fears. Humans are crave to be liked. Hence you always seek approval of others. You are not afraid of others feelings. You are afraid of your own feelings due to your inability of managing your own emotions. You do not have any purpose, Just you do what others are doing, you don't want to do what you want to be doing. Human personality is continuously evolving and keeps changing with time. Personality is not one rather it is multi facet depending up on circumstances. You will become automatically powerful when you are aware of your strengths and weaknesses

♣♣♣(46)♣♣♣

Vision without all facts is a mirage leads nowhere. A goal should scare less and excite more. Plan prevents confusion. Do only what you can do. Never attempt to do what you can't do else it will remain incomplete. You should be clear of what you really want. Never have unrealistic expectations about your capability.

♣♣♣(47)♣♣♣

Never judge by others opinion.

♣♣♣(48)♣♣♣

Humans are designed by God to do only one task at any time. If you try to indulge in multitasking you will be surely forced to procrastinate.

♣♠♣(49)♣♠♣
Criticize people in private never in public. We love complaining
about others rather connecting to others.
♣♠♣(50)♣♠♣
If you take care of your present, automatically it cares your
future. Do not let one part of failure to paralyze whole.
Progress is essential to exist. Masking truth doesn't help to
Progress. No struggles no Progress. Progress is race in-
between desires and purposes. Biggest problem in life (in
profession and personal life is you know how to move forward
but still stuck as you are more attached to self serving. The
moment you stop accepting excuses you begin your progress.
♣♠♣(51)♣♠♣
Your future needs you, your past doesn't.
♣♠♣(52)♣♠♣
You can resort to risk only if you can afford consequences of it's
risk outcome. Never risking is even risking more. Risk is as
exiting as you think as fearful as you feel. When we believe in
ourselves we are capable of taking risks.
♣♠♣(53)♣♠♣
World is full of people with desires. Most people are concerned
for their own heart. Self care is not selfishness it is sometimes
essential. People are selfish souls with happy masks. Don't get
too attached.
♣♠♣(54)♣♠♣
Good attitude converts negative stress into positive stress.
♣♠♣(55)♣♠♣
Your happiness is nowhere it is inside you.
♣♠♣(56)♣♠♣
Your proactive reaction to stress hurts you not stress.
♣♠♣(57)♣♠♣
To be successful you need to be out of your comfort zone and
do what is right to do. Success is a reality when we make our
decisions for the person we have become. Failure converts to
success when you learn from it.

♣♣♣*(58)*♣♣♣

People who possess wisdom are unaffected by negativity and pessimism. Most of the people do not know how to connect with people, it does not mean they are negative people. All your negativity sprouts from your unprocessed emotions.

When we are unable to process and understand some emotions, they are converted into our negative emotions. Our negative feelings pile up continuously, pressurizing internally resulting in sudden out bursts and sensitivity to external environment. Our pessimism ruins our lives more than others.

♣♣♣*(59)*♣♣♣

Thinking, thinking, thinking, thinking, we are all lost in and by thinking. Unless intervened and stopped thinking is going to be un ending. Thinking has to be stopped at right time and right moment.

♣♣♣*(60)*♣♣♣

You are more confused than ever before. You are confused because you don't want understand or you don't understand. Root cause to confusion is either lack of clarity or lack of understanding.

♣♣♣*(61)*♣♣♣

You are fond of creating prejudices with your limited experiences. You very well know your prejudices are biased. But your heart compels to switch off your mind and by heart to follow your prejudices. Your preexisting beliefs and prejudices never allow you to realize your full potential. Preexisting beliefs mostly illogical and holds you back.

♣♣♣*(62)*♣♣♣

We are afraid to remain alone. Hence we always try to seek approval of others.

People's irrational and unpredictable behavior is directed by their subconscious core commitment. Their behavior continues to prevail till core commitment is addressed.

♣♣♣*(63)*♣♣♣

People think unknown as discomfort.

We always try to seek only what we know. Whatever be the circumstances we are in we always try to bring back we are comfortable with. Humans are guided by objective of comfort. We tend to resist any thing outside realm of comfort till assured. Mind is vulnerable to deception, it interprets familiarity as good and comfort. We are discomfortable in present moment as we are attached to past or future.

♣♣♣(64)♣♣♣

We limit our beliefs because we want to keep ourselves safe.

♣♣♣(65)♣♣♣

It's natural law good and bad coexist, there cannot be either good alone or bad alone.

♣♣♣(66)♣♣♣

True healing is shifting our attitude the way we think.

♣♣♣(67)♣♣♣

Most of the times we are hurt by ourselves due to our own self protectionism.

♣♣♣(68)♣♣♣

Though failures are normal in life but you have to accept the responsibility for failures occurring due to wrong reasons. Failing due to negligence will irreversibly pull you back.

♣♣♣(69)♣♣♣

Our life style depends upon people with whom we spend with in our lives. Humans are designed to survive in nature by responding to impulses of nature. However they are suffering from mental and physical trauma due to synthetic Impulses generated by modern lifestyle.

♣♣♣(70)♣♣♣

Build and be with a circle of people who inspire you and support you.

♣♣♣(71)♣♣♣

We trust our doubts more than our abilities.

♣♣♣(72)♣♣♣

Your ability or talent are only limited. You can't be master of everything.

Focus your attention only on few things that matter most to you.

♣♣♣(73)♣♣♣

Anger is a reveals our boundaries as well as what we care about. True anger triggers change.

♣♣♣(74)♣♣♣

We can't change other the way we want. Focus on others for what we can learn from their behavior. You never live your real life when you look your life through the eyes of others. Others will give access to their mind only to trusted ones. You can influence for change in others when you can access their subconscious mind bypassing their conscious mind.

♣♣♣(75)♣♣♣

When something is wrong it brings confusion in you due to silent fight in between your mind and heart. When you make wrong thing as right thing into your life you will suffer from irresolvable chronic trauma. Trauma occurs when fear wins over you. Suffering gives value to life.

♣♣♣(76)♣♣♣

Self healing starts when you bring back your mind and body to your most natural state. You can't ignore your wounds, they need your attention as well as healing

♣♣♣(77)♣♣♣

When you don't understand you over think. Our mind thinking is unending till mind understands. Your capacity to control your thoughts indicates your social integration.

♣♣♣(78)♣♣♣

When you prepare you don't worry.

♣♣♣(79)♣♣♣

Deep breathing reduces anxiety and enables focus.

♣♣♣(80)♣♣♣

Stress is generated due to unmanageable challenge or threat.

♣♣♣(81)♣♣♣

Stress reduces ability to be creative and innovate.

♣♣♣(82)♣♣♣

Stress increases exponentially under unpredictable and uncertain circumstances. Outcome in stressful situations is unpredictable.

♣♣♣(83)♣♣♣

Only weak men are addicted. Every form of addiction is bad.

♣♣♣(84)♣♣♣

Learn from lessons of distress. Suffering happens to everyone in this world only timing is different. Suffering makes us as humans. Adversity reveals leadership talent. Measure of man is by what he stands at the time of adversity.

♣♣♣(85)♣♣♣

There is no use in arguing with the inevitable. Remember argument is just like a overcoat.. A merry heart keeps you happy and stress free.

♣♣♣(86)♣♣♣

Your analysis may never end by your paralysis by analysis. Hence you need to self limit your desire.

♣♣♣(87)♣♣♣

Anxiety is created when you want to take action without taking responsibility for consequences.

♣♣♣(88)♣♣♣

Remember success is uncertain as it depends upon many external factors other than you. Hence never ever certainly expect and never get disappointed by failure.

♣♣♣(89)♣♣♣

Non honest doubts drains your energy and time.

♣♣♣(90)♣♣♣

Reality of fear is less severe than your imagination. Wisdom can conquer fear.

♣♣♣(91)♣♣♣

Most people think that everything they can do themselves, that is an illusion. However Expert you may be you can't do everything for yourself, it delays too much and causes enormous stress as well as results in imperfection.

Progress and productivity can happen only with delegation and team work. Hence resort to delegation wherever possible.

♣♣♣(92)♣♣♣

There is lot of difference between theory and practice and plan and reality. Always while executing you have to have practical approach. You can't always insist for being right always blindly sticking to your plan or theory. Try to have optimum approach.

♣♣♣(93)♣♣♣

Sex creates powerful biological bond. It is difficult to predict appropriateness of bond, hence sex alone can create enormous stress due to this biological bond. Never indulge in direct sexual relationship with anyone. First evaluate and know your partner and establish emotional bonding. It will be perfect bliss, joy and happiness in the union of emotional bonding and physical bonding.

♣♣♣(94)♣♣♣

Whether it is your personal life or professional life boundaries are important. In a life time you can have only finite relationships. Everyone need not know you. Your life can't be thrown open to everyone that creates too much disturbance in your life. Having boundaries creates respect. Having boundaries is honoring your self. Creating boundaries maintains and ensures your values. Setting boundaries enable you to gain your personal power. Most of the men find difficulty in setting their boundaries.

♣♣♣(95)♣♣♣

When you really live with your balanced feelings you are powerful, assertive and energized.

However in life all live life pressurized by bottling up their feelings being afraid of others feelings. When you bottle up your feelings remaining unexpressed, pressure builds up it triggers out of control emotional out bursts spoiling your relationships.

♣♣♣(96)♣♣♣

Your life as peaceful as it is related to reality.

When you live away from reality your life is full of lies, illusions, confusion and chaotic. Reality alone can give stability and tranquility to your mind.

♣♣♣(97)♣♣♣

In life we encounter situations either we can control or situations that are beyond our control. Just surrender to situations that are beyond your control. When you surrender to uncontrollable situation then only you will be fully aware of situation and you will be knowing how to tackle the consequences. Once you surrender that gives ways to new opportunities. When you try to confront and control uncontrollable situations it gives enormous disturbance internally and externally and you can never achieve your objectives. You will also waste your valuable time and resources.

♣♣♣(98)♣♣♣

Chaos is order of nature. Human existence itself is chaotic. Life is never smooth. Life is filled with experiences that are uncertain, unpredictable and beyond your or others control. Having smooth expectations from Life will make you frustrated.

♣♣♣(99)♣♣♣

Never help people with strings attached. Never have expectations in return when you help others. Helping others is human existence as man is social animal. If you attach strings others betrayal can cause enormous pain to you.

♣♣♣(100)♣♣♣

Never pretend to be needless by hiding your needs. This will result in unfulfilled desire that makes you act in irrational ways.

♣♣♣(101)♣♣♣

Always keep your priorities above others priorities. If you can't give importance to your self who else will care you and bother you. If others hijack your importance, your life remains disturbed.

♣♣♣(102)♣♣♣

Never depend upon approval of others for everything you do.

only know yourself well. Everyone has biases, prejudices and no one can really know your situation well other than you. You are only best judge for your self. Have courage and develop confidence to take decisions that matters in your life. When you depend on others approval others are controlling your life not you.

♣♣♣(103)♣♣♣

Learn to please yourself first. You can't please everyone if you do so you will end up pleasing no one. Many people try to project themselves being good by putting effort for pleasing everyone. Ultimately, that results in strained relationships as trust in you is lost. Your efforts will boomerang in negative way. External validation by consensus will never achieve anything. Moreover this will more complicate things.

♣♣♣(104)♣♣♣

Man is a social animal. If you do not have social connections it give enormous stress. People are not attracted to perfect or good people. People seek people for shared interests, shared problems and to individuals thriving energy.

♣♣♣(105)♣♣♣

Every individual has his own mental model about others individuals or activities/things based of his experiences, prejudices, external circumstances, internal factors and inputs. No two individuals perception truly matches perfectly. Hence when anyone disagrees with your opinion don't be panic don't argue, listen to him carefully, think rationally, counter him with logic and reason.

People's heart can be won only by logic. Remember no one is ideally perfect in perception, just they are perfect perception limited only to their model.

♣♣♣(106)♣♣♣

There is no good man or bad man. Man is an integrated man with qualities power, assertiveness, courage, passions, imperfections, mistakes.

Hence never divide your human interactions as good or bad, just treat them as just momentary instants of life and continue your relationships.

♣♣♣(107)♣♣♣

Frustrations are created when don't act with your own intuitions and conscience. If you keep on going accumulating frustrations in life, one day they will pop up like a relief valve of a pressure cooker.
Never try to undermine your intuitions or conscience.
When you try to hide your needs, emotions and mistakes frustration develops.

♣♣♣(108)♣♣♣

Body and mind are rigidly coupled like computer software and hardware. Disturbance in one affects the other. More than 95% of illnesses are thought to have direct or indirect psychological origin. Our individual inability to cope stress causes disease.

♣♣♣(109)♣♣♣

Stress does not affect directly. The way people change in response to stress affects directly productivity and quality.
Stress is expensive to individual and organization.

♣♣♣(110)♣♣♣

Modern day stress happens in minds. Stress is mostly created due to imagination rather reality.

♣♣♣(111)♣♣♣

Unmanaged stress can create cascading disturbances like ripples in water in a never ending loop. This propagates further diseases and can go out of control without timely intervention.

♣♣♣(112)♣♣♣

Positive imagination has healing power over stress.
But negative imagination can create enormous stress.
Imagination is most powerful God's gift to humans.

♣♣♣(113)♣♣♣

Workaholics are created due to chronic stress. Workaholics are useful only for short-term.

♣♣♣(114)♣♣♣

Drinking alcohol never reduces stress. All decisions done under alcohol are wrong.

♣♣♣(115)♣♣♣

Some are more vulnerable to stress than others. These factors can make you vulnerable, Low self esteem, low confidence, personal problems, adjustment, changes, empty lives.

♣♣♣(116)♣♣♣

Sleep disturbances are common result of stress.

♣♣♣(117)♣♣♣

Expectations, roles and responsibilities must be clearly mentioned across organizations structure.

♣♣♣(118)♣♣♣

Thank you to everyone and everything in life. That reduces stress.

♣♣♣(119)♣♣♣

When when to start and stop activity in your life.

♣♣♣(120)♣♣♣

Be happy and receive others with smile.
Your response will also be in same manner.

♣♣♣(121)♣♣♣

There shouldn't be authority without responsibility and responsibility without authority.

♣♣♣(122)♣♣♣

Define Your life not in Negatives but with Positives.

♣♣♣(123)♣♣♣

Learn to say NO when ever required.

♣♣♣(124)♣♣♣

Learn to forgive people in life.

♣♣♣(125)♣♣♣

When required learn to ask for help of others.

♣♣♣(126)♣♣♣

Daily short duration gentle exercises releases stress coping hormones and keep you healthy.

♣♣♣(127)♣♣♣

Create your own custom made environment to suit to your personality.

♣♣♣(128)♣♣♣

Relax some times.

♣♣♣(129)♣♣♣

Never communicate indirectly, always talk directly to concern either face to face or over phone.

♣♣♣(130)♣♣♣

Criticism must be constructive and not in public. Criticism should also contain element of praise.

♣♣♣(131)♣♣♣

Learn new skills time to time updated.

♣♣♣(132)♣♣♣

Make provision for people to express their anger or emotions.

♣♣♣(133)♣♣♣

Take break and go on holidays.

♣♣♣(134)♣♣♣

Modern humans evolved gradually over thousands of years for adopting to the environment they live. But modern environment has changed for rapidly than our bodies evolved. That is why our mind and body couldn't cope with modern environment.

♣♣♣(135)♣♣♣

Every moment of our lives filled with problems, anxieties, fears and crises. But nothing is harming life. But all are affecting the way you live. Our responses to our modern environment is primitive. These outdated responses cause enormous stress in us due to mismatch between stimulants and responses resulting in disturbed mind and body.

♣♣♣(136)♣♣♣

Our modern body design is same as that of the primitive man roaming forests. Our modern body response to stress is the same way as that of primitive human, nothing changed. Primitive man faced stress due to few problems where as modern man is facing with too many problems.

Problems many be too many but the body response to stress is same old fashion in single way.

♣♣♣(137)♣♣♣

Stress is part of life. No one is immune or resistant stress damage. There is no super human.

♣♣♣(138)♣♣♣

Stress is like a tip of iceberg. It's effects are 99% submerged.

♣♣♣(139)♣♣♣

For healthy life you need to have good relationships. All relationships are with some sort of reciprocal expectations, whether it is emotional or other. The problem comes when you can't get away your bad relationships. Get rid of non workable relationships and move on.

♣♣♣(140)♣♣♣

Physical exercises, breathing exercises like pranayamam, sports, playing with kids, counseling, reading, watching TV, having emotional bond with women, learning, meditation, living in nature, natural diet, mindfulness, traveling, teaching, social work, social gathering, hobbies and natural lifestyle helps in reducing stress.

♣♣♣(141)♣♣♣

Every human do have failures and weaknesses. The problem is rather focusing on your strengths everyone tries to spend their valuable time on failures and weaknesses.. This creates further problems as well as worsening condition further.

♣♣♣(142)♣♣♣

Decision making is one of the main cause for stress in our personal and professional lives.

♣♣♣(143)♣♣♣

Decision making consumes lot of energy.
Hence segregated the problems into routine and non routine problems. Use predefined auto solution procedures for handling unimportant and routine problems. This saves your time and energy.

Put your genuine efforts and energy for addressing non routine and important problems. Once you put your energy and efforts on unimportant and routine problems they consume and control your life.

♣♣♣(144)♣♣♣

Whenever you find exhausted in any activity stop the activity for a while do some thing interesting the immerse you fully as well as fun, relaxing and pleasant.

♣♣♣(145)♣♣♣

Micro managing is one of the diseases we suffer, we try to fiddle our activities and projects frequently, thus rather helping further this adversely affects the activities due to too frequent corrections.

♣♣♣(146)♣♣♣

Don't be too theoretical, Only include your workable actions as a part of your planning.

♣♣♣(147)♣♣♣

Time for achieving perfectionism is infinite and difficult to estimate or account. Hence try to focus on improving your processes and skills rather focusing on perfectionism.

♣♣♣(148)♣♣♣

When you compare with others that will create doubt in your abilities creating stress and anxiety. Instead analyze your past performance and focus on improving future performance.

♣♣♣(149)♣♣♣

No miracle can happen over night. Have positive attitude, believe in your self, appreciate your progress and efforts. At least try to progress in small steps. Break big tasks into small tasks. Tackle small tasks.

♣♣♣(150)♣♣♣

Stress is unknowingly adds to life. Hence you must have methods for managing stress to suit to your personality. Stress shouldn't intervene with your personal and professional lives. You need to experiment and find out suitable techniques that eliminates stress in your life.

♣♣♣(151)♣♣♣

People assume different views in different circumstances during different times. This is not an abnormality.

♣♣♣(152)♣♣♣

Stress removes synergy in your life.
Stress drains your life's energy levels. You will be not in a position to focus your energies to the purpose. Though you got power you will become powerless.

♣♣♣(153)♣♣♣

You can't remover stressors from your life. However only option left for you in life is managing stressors such that they can affect you least.

♣♣♣(154)♣♣♣

Life is full of problems whether it is personal or professional lives. You have to solve your problems to live, there is no escape. Many times you face unsolvable problems beyond your ability to find solutions. Just take rest, relax, play or sleep forget problems for some time and comeback, your brain automatically give creative insight solutions to the problem.

♣♣♣(155)♣♣♣

When we are under stressful conditions, our body will secrete stress causing some hormones(epinephrine, norepinephrine, cortosol. These hormones will shutdown brains normal functions and switches brain to bypass mode only maintaining only body's essential functions. Your rational thinking and subconscious mind will be stopped. Your body will act in self protection mode. This process will be analogies to safe mode in computer when there is problem in computer. Where you will be able to do minimum functions. In human body this is called flight or fight mode. Human body is designed for this flight or fight mode only for short durations.   But in modern lifestyle humans are living in stressful conditions for prolonged period. This is causing irreversible damage to human mind and body.

♣♣♣(156)♣♣♣

When we relax, stay in calm environment, do rejuvenating activities body releases stress countering hormones (endorphins, dopamine). These hormones create feelings of well being and sense of tranquility in brain.

♣♣♣(157)♣♣♣

Relaxation enables creativity, new insights, performance, solutions, resilience.

♣♣♣(158)♣♣♣

For regenerating mind, while putting peak efforts break suddenly for some time and relax.

♣♣♣(159)♣♣♣

Your relaxation will get initiated only when you detach and ignore your stress creating thoughts.

♣♣♣(160)♣♣♣

chronic stress results disabilities of, choosing priorities, decision making, time management, misunderstanding, inability to learn, fear, anxiety, impatience, anger, panic. Chronic stress is not a illness, it is your continuous response to circumstances in a negative way.

♣♣♣(161)♣♣♣

Replace your negative thinking with positive thinking.

♣♣♣(162)♣♣♣

When you pursue stressful work, take break every few hours and spend some time face to face with person you like.

♣♣♣(163)♣♣♣

Stress simultaneously overloads entire brain just jamming brain.

♣♣♣(164)♣♣♣

Physical isolation causes stress. Human to human interactions reduces stress effectively not by texting or talking over phone.

♣♣♣(165)♣♣♣

People addicted with carbohydrate diet suffer from blood glucose fluctuations that impairs or disturbs some brain functions.

♣♣♣(166)♣♣♣

Physical exercises secretes some good brain hormones that help in maintaining brain chemistry and fight stress.

♣♣♣(167)♣♣♣

You have choose work the way that suits to your personality. Everyone's way of work is unique.

♣♣♣(168)♣♣♣

When you are stresses try to keep out for some time, ask questions, divert your self by doing some documentation work or interesting work, talk to your friends.

♣♣♣(169)♣♣♣

Omega3 diets or capsules found to create better brain chemistry that helps in reducing stress. You need to consult your physician for guidance.

♣♣♣(170)♣♣♣

Take balanced diet.

♣♣♣(171)♣♣♣

Adequate sleep is essential.

♣♣♣(172)♣♣♣

Create a culture of trust and authentic communication.

♣♣♣(173)♣♣♣

Dispose clutter on your table frequently.

♣♣♣(174)♣♣♣

Have quiet time break for calming your brain.

♣♣♣(175)♣♣♣

Handle your emails only at few scheduled times of day.

♣♣♣(176)♣♣♣

Every evening based on today's feedback plan activities for next day.

♣♣♣(177)♣♣♣

Handle hard work, important work only in the morning when your energy is highest.

♣♣♣(178)♣♣♣

Enjoy your activities with background music.

♣♣♣(179)♣♣♣

You can have exercise break in office by moving uptown stairs.

♣♣♣(180)♣♣♣
Delegation is one of the effective ways to reduce stress.
♣♣♣(181)♣♣♣
Work pressure seeks fast thinking rather deep thinking causing
anxiety.
♣♣♣(182)♣♣♣
Mismatch between your skills and tasks can cause stress and
anxiety.
♣♣♣(183)♣♣♣
Appreciate people around you, that creates positive vibes
around you.
♣♣♣(184)♣♣♣
Have small meals every few hours.
♣♣♣(185)♣♣♣
Deep breathing helps in getting away negative thoughts.
♣♣♣(186)♣♣♣
Pool your time and energies towards activities that are most
important to you.
♣♣♣(187)♣♣♣
Have some tine for self reflection.
♣♣♣(188)♣♣♣
Carryout important work distractions free.
♣♣♣(189)♣♣♣
Keep someone to mentor and guide you.
♣♣♣(190)♣♣♣
When you control your emotions that will improve
effectiveness and efficiency of your energy spending.
♣♣♣(191)♣♣♣
Positive emotions can sustain only for short duration and
negative emotions prevail continuously endlessly.
Hence you gave to motivate continuously for generating
positive emotions.
♣♣♣(192)♣♣♣
Facts are facts. But their perception depends upon individual
interpretation.

You can't act on multiple goals simultaneously.

Develop positive habits regularly.

know and manage your boundaries.

Have and follow daily to do lists for your activities .

First step to detox your mind is you have to break negativity ever repeating loop chain. For that you have to choose few rhyming words like a mantra and start repeatedly pronouncing these rhyming words like a loop. Once you do this repeated rhyming automatically you will replace your negative thinking loop.

Second step to detox mind is stop thinking. Continue with your repeated rhyming and simultaneously try to focus on your breathing or externally on any imaginary focal point. Slowly increase depth of your focus from macro level to micro level until you have created a condition of unique absolute thoughtlessness or stillness or tranquility.

Third step to detox after coming out of stillness, replace all your thinking with only positive and constructive thoughts.

Fourth step to detox is being and staying mindful, whatever you do only thinking of present moment and living in the present.

Fifth step to detox is practice any one type of breathing exercise for few minutes daily like pranayamam. This will tranquilize your mind and recharges. There are lot of scientific and non scientific breathing exercises available openly follow any one of them.

These breathing exercises you can do at any place or posture of your convenience. Breathing exercise helps to remain mindful, focused and energetic.

♣♣♣(202)♣♣♣

Nuts and seeds repairs as well as keeps your mind healthy due to presence of omega3 fatty acids and other nutrients. However you have to consume limited quantity daily. Avoid raw nuts and seeds and consume only after soaking them in water over night. You can change nut types periodically.

♣♣♣(203)♣♣♣

Add spiritual component to your life. Spirituality gives you clarity, confidence and mental peace. Spirituality is a necessity for humans. Goodness of spirituality is proven for thousands of years. Spirituality is one of the very good detoxing antidote and it enables being mindful.

♣♣♣(204)♣♣♣

Mental peace comes from true self realization. Self realization is true state of life. Doubts are mental agitation. Doubts are cleared by being mindful. Doubt creates mental toxins.

♣♣♣(205)♣♣♣

Many forms of Meditation is available. You can choose any one of them that suits you. Meditation generates life energy and force.

♣♣♣(206)♣♣♣

Keep cool and clam in everyday of life. This restraint is essential in hectic modern life. You can't change or make things happen overnight. Things takes their own time whether you feel for them or not.

♣♣♣(207)♣♣♣

When you play with kids are pets that relaxes you and detoxes your mental toxins. They are playful and innocent soothing your heart and mind with deep impact.

♣♣♣(208)♣♣♣

Negativity is the main mental toxin of mind.

Pessimism is a seed & behaves like a exponential triggered chain reaction cascading and propagating like ripples in water. Negativity is a closed loop continuously repeating and creating ever increasing ripples.

♣♣♣(209)♣♣♣

Modern lifestyle is so hectic and busy that makes you more mechanical like a robot. You will not be in a position to use your mind or heart effectively and efficiently. Self reflection is essential to regenerate your mind and heart to make them productive. Time to time detach yourself from your surroundings and leave space for self reflection and feeling in a calm environment.

♣♣♣(210)♣♣♣

When humans started living as nuclear families from joint families they became individualistic and selfish.
Due to lack of others emotional support they started indulging in self talk and comparing themselves with others. They lost ability to think for common good and good for others. Modern humans don't think everyone is unique and lost the ability assess self-worth and stared indulging in negative self talk. Imaginary feelings of lack of self worth is the main reason for creation of mental toxins. Let go pessimistic self talk. Feel good about self. It is not that easy to let self remove self talk, just replace it with constructive thoughts.

♣♣♣(211)♣♣♣

Most of the people are stuck in endless arguments trying to enforce their point of view. In this process they get mentally disturbed resulting in accumulation of mental toxins. Please realize whether you accept or not truth will always prevails. The root cause of the problem is everyone rather addressing the problem tries to attack individual ego. Though there may be real solution to the problem, however there is a problem of acceptance by all due to adversely affected some parties.

Hence ego clash do occurs between all. Best thing to avoid confrontation is to find a solution in between real solution to solution for common good.

♣♣♣(212)♣♣♣

Anger creates delusion. Anger and intolerance are twins. Fruit if anger is a bad consequences.

♣♣♣(213)♣♣♣

Your anger is a cruel punishment you give it to self.

♣♣♣(214)♣♣♣

You can't see your true world when you are anger.

♣♣♣(215)♣♣♣

Angry persons are emotionally stupid. Anger generates destructive emotions.

♣♣♣(216)♣♣♣

There is a prevailing dormant pain underneath an anger. Anger is a reaction to pain.

♣♣♣(217)♣♣♣

Anger is a triggered protection of personality. Angry person will becomes emotionally stupid.

♣♣♣(218)♣♣♣

When you are calm people don't know where and what to attack, because there is known indication.

♣♣♣(219)♣♣♣

Refrain from action and speech when you're angry. Anger is sign of weakness.

♣♣♣(220)♣♣♣

Constructive anger can become a catalyst for change.

♣♣♣(221)♣♣♣

People who are capable of making you anger are controlling you. You loose your conscience when angry.

♣♣♣(222)♣♣♣

Controlling emotions of anger and frustrations is crucial for progress and achievement in life.

♣♣♣(223)♣♣♣

Conflict are common, unavoidable and not preventable.

♣♣♣*(224)*♣♣♣
Most find skewed solutions for conflicts, momentarily
forgetting their goals for a while.

♣♣♣*(225)*♣♣♣
Conflict is not good versus bad, but it is one man's beliefs
versus another man's beliefs.

♣♣♣*(226)*♣♣♣
Conflict is a war inside you & and is battle of himself. You can
never win a conflict by onside force.

♣♣♣*(227)*♣♣♣
Peace is ability to manage conflict but not escaping from
conflict. Love all including our enemies, however whomsoever
we fight we must protect our own interests.

♣♣♣*(228)*♣♣♣
Conflicts are built-up due to avoidance and autocratic thinking.
Caution, some are interested to keep conflicts alive just to
create history.

♣♣♣*(229)*♣♣♣
Root cause of most of the Conflicts lies in our fundamental
assumptions of the issue. You can't understand conflicts when
your heart is unopened.

♣♣♣*(230)*♣♣♣
Conflicts avoidance disconnects us and indirectly affects
productivity. Avoidance of conflict further aggravates the issue.

♣♣♣*(231)*♣♣♣
Real conflict is in-between your heart and mind. Honest
conversations could fix many conflicts. One can't work with two
interests simultaneously. When your heart wins over your
mind you won the Conflict.

♣♣♣*(232)*♣♣♣
Escalation of Conflict increases your ignorance, that makes you
isolated from reality and truth. Conflict is a difference between
your history and your plans.

♣♣♣*(233)*♣♣♣

Biased solutions for conflicts drifts your plan from main course permanently, making you never able to achieve your goals. Resolution of conflicts for mutual benefit enables trust and reliability.

♣♣♣(234)♣♣♣

Ego kills your relationships, your talents and your growth. You can't meet your highest self with ego.

♣♣♣(235)♣♣♣

Ego develops when you live in separation with others.

♣♣♣(236)♣♣♣

Avoid those who defend their ego and offend your soul.

♣♣♣(237)♣♣♣

Trust is inversely proportional to ego.

♣♣♣(238)♣♣♣

Your ego prevents you from becoming greatest or successful. Ego beyond threshold kills your talent.

♣♣♣(239)♣♣♣

Ego is what he was. Egoist is someone telling about themselves that you are forced to listen without judgment. Ego denies others reality.

♣♣♣(240)♣♣♣

More the knowledge you acquire less the ego you possess.

♣♣♣(241)♣♣♣

Your imprisoned cage is your ego. Ego is your illusion of yourself.

♣♣♣(242)♣♣♣

Ego makes you feel nothing is more important than you. Ego is one sort of self created elevated threshold yourself respect.

♣♣♣(243)♣♣♣

Love and friendship can only melt ego. In ego versus love, most of the time ego dominates.

♣♣♣(244)♣♣♣

Egoist as a leader if unchecked can sink a ship of whole team. Egoism is a self tranquilizer that makes you insensitive to others feelings.

♣♣♣*(245)*♣♣♣
If you have heart, there is a room for everything.
♣♣♣*(246)*♣♣♣
Make best impression on heart of your personnel.
♣♣♣*(247)*♣♣♣
Encourage informal gathering of personnel for bondage.
♣♣♣*(248)*♣♣♣
You can't just ignore emotions of your personnel.
♣♣♣*(249)*♣♣♣
Simple human touch enables to be more productive with least effort.
♣♣♣*(250)*♣♣♣
Help people with behavior problems with counseling.
♣♣♣*(251)*♣♣♣
If you surrender to emotions of others you can never be productive. Emotions are impulsive.
♣♣♣*(252)*♣♣♣
Unaddressed emotions can seed stress and unhappiness.
♣♣♣*(253)*♣♣♣
Memory of emotional experience is prolonged.
♣♣♣*(254)*♣♣♣
Your emotions are you, reflections of you. Main reason for most of human actions is emotion.
♣♣♣*(255)*♣♣♣
You can quench others emotions just by making them to understand.
♣♣♣*(256)*♣♣♣
Failure is delayed achievement not a defeat. Failure is a detour. Fear of failure is major cause of failures.
♣♣♣*(257)*♣♣♣
We can never prevent probability of failures, however we can minimize effect of failure consequences.
♣♣♣*(258)*♣♣♣
Failure is due to doing things not exactly right. Failure is inability to practice practically one's own experience.

♣♣♣(259)♣♣♣

Failure is inevitable when you try to please everyone. When you try to convince everyone it's a compromise for failure.

♣♣♣(260)♣♣♣

People think more of what others think of their failures rather about their failure. You can learn consequences of failure only when you accept failures.

♣♣♣(261)♣♣♣

Failure is not a mistake. Failure is ones throttled optimal performance limited by circumstances.

♣♣♣(262)♣♣♣

If you avoid failure you will also avoid success, because road is same.

♣♣♣(263)♣♣♣

Failure is beginning afresh. Failure is a part of success. Failure builds strong character.

♣♣♣(264)♣♣♣

Only difference between success and failure is ability. Failure is a reality when you stop trying.

♣♣♣(265)♣♣♣

Failure is a leadership confusion in deciding what is important to all. Most people are preoccupied with insignificant thinking.

♣♣♣(266)♣♣♣

Excuses are foundation stone for a house of failures. Excuses never achieved anything great.

♣♣♣(267)♣♣♣

Don't decide your future out of fear. Look beyond fear, you will find your alternatives for a solution.

♣♣♣(268)♣♣♣

Fear is created out of ignorance. You fear melts away when you try to understand.

♣♣♣(269)♣♣♣

Fear of unknown is the main reason for procrastination.

♣♣♣(270)♣♣♣

You start growing the moment you have overcome your fear.

♣♣♣(271)♣♣♣
Fear creates illusion, magnifies things and stops life. Fear limits us.

♣♣♣(272)♣♣♣
Most people are defeated by their fears rather by competition.

♣♣♣(273)♣♣♣
What you really wanted is there beyond your fear. Hence you must confront your fear.

♣♣♣(274)♣♣♣
You can overcome your fears when you are master of your mind but not when mind mastered you.

♣♣♣(275)♣♣♣
Working with ethics & integrity leaves no room for fear.

♣♣♣(276)♣♣♣
Your suffering is proportional to your fear but not to the reality.

♣♣♣(277)♣♣♣
Fear is expensive than failure. It's a good teacher.

♣♣♣(278)♣♣♣
Success depends upon your ability to perceive the present .i.e. mindfulness.

♣♣♣(279)♣♣♣
When you live in present every moment will be creative.

♣♣♣(280)♣♣♣
Mindfulness makes space, creates infinite capacity.

♣♣♣(281)♣♣♣
When you live in present your understanding increases and thinking disappears.

♣♣♣(282)♣♣♣
Mindfulness defeats prejudice.

♣♣♣(283)♣♣♣
You can only find solutions when you live in present.

♣♣♣(284)♣♣♣
Mindfulness realizes your full potential.

♣♣♣(285)♣♣♣
Mindfulness keeps you fit and healthy.

♣♣♣(286)♣♣♣
Mindful people exhibit true and original personality without being hijacked by thoughts and prejudice.
♣♣♣(287)♣♣♣
Mindfulness makes you feel good you.
♣♣♣(288)♣♣♣
You will become magnetic when you live in present.
♣♣♣(289)♣♣♣
Life is a succession of lessons being learnt from successes and failures.

Problems are generated by 1.only thinking, thinking; 2.Not thinking. Everyone do have problems, however only some people are capable of challenging them.
♣♣♣(290)♣♣♣
Wisdom prevents suffering from past failures. If it is inevitable problem try to minimize your losses. Competitive spirit destroys all feelings of human fraternity and cooperation.
♣♣♣(291)♣♣♣
When you accept failure you will start learning for success. Never look back to history but don't repeat historical failures.
♣♣♣(292)♣♣♣
You can never solve problems on your own, however you can think of alternate solutions. If you are positive in a negative situation, you win.
♣♣♣(293)♣♣♣
Look the issue in 360 degree in every aspect.
Use closed questions to reveal information.
with questions till you reach answers.
♣♣♣(294)♣♣♣
Set time limits for realization of the problem based on priority.
Act timely as soon as possible.
If problem is really important to you, you will surely find a way out.
♣♣♣(295)♣♣♣

Unhappy persons are the source for revealing serious problems. Never judge by others opinions. Many problems are created by our imagination.

♣♣♣(296)♣♣♣

If you bring unsolved problems up they treat you as if you are not doing your job. Sugar coating the past will always come back to you as problem.

♣♣♣(297)♣♣♣

Don't imagine answers concentrate on questions to find solutions, use previous experience of others to find solutions. Over thinking creates new problems.

♣♣♣(298)♣♣♣

Know which question to ask for getting right answer. Think about the answer you received but not about the person answering. Distinguish between work related problems and personal problems.

♣♣♣(299)♣♣♣

Before arriving at final solution you should possess complete facts. Look for the positive side in the situation. When everything is uncertain anything is possible.

♣♣♣(300)♣♣♣

Acceptance of consequences of bold achievement.

♣♣♣(301)♣♣♣

Opportunity and risk coexist.

♣♣♣(302)♣♣♣

Risk is as exiting as you think and as fearful as you feel. Risk taking depends on your attitude.

♣♣♣(303)♣♣♣

Biggest risk is not taking any risk under uncertainty.

♣♣♣(304)♣♣♣

Never risking is even risking more.

♣♣♣(305)♣♣♣

Progress includes taking risks as and when required.

♣♣♣(306)♣♣♣

No risk no miracle.

♣♣♣(307)♣♣♣
Challenges are hurdles in achieving goals.
♣♣♣(308)♣♣♣
Challenge is a risk.
♣♣♣(309)♣♣♣
You can resort to risk only if you can afford consequences of it's risk outcome.
♣♣♣(310)♣♣♣
Risk taking is like swimming in water you will be never knowing depth of water, you are dependent only on your ability to survive.
♣♣♣(311)♣♣♣
People with temporary flash memory are only happy people.
♣♣♣(312)♣♣♣
To remain happy never think of others. Happiness makes you ignorant.
♣♣♣(313)♣♣♣
When you are happy others too will be happy.
♣♣♣(314)♣♣♣
Happiness is only transitional.
♣♣♣(315)♣♣♣
Happiness is highly contagious and creates positive vibrations all around.
♣♣♣(316)♣♣♣
Shared happiness will spread & increase multifold like rapid mutations of living cells.
♣♣♣(317)♣♣♣
Happiness = results − expectations.
♣♣♣(318)♣♣♣
Happiness is as good as your mindset.
♣♣♣(319)♣♣♣
Synchronized melody of Love, Work and Hope together sustains happiness throughout your life.
♣♣♣(320)♣♣♣
Happiness is triggered naturally.

♣♣♣*(321)*♣♣♣
Don't let your sensitivity to disturb you happiness when not required.

♣♣♣*(322)*♣♣♣
Nothing can be more influential than money. Money makes immediate and quick impact. Money kills most of the human problems of modern world.

♣♣♣*(323)*♣♣♣
Investing money makes you richer but not by saving money. You can make more money from money only.

♣♣♣*(324)*♣♣♣
Don't let people IN, in decisions that you can't afford. Small changes to your routine spending add upto significant savings. You can be richer by limiting your desires.

♣♣♣*(325)*♣♣♣
Normal human beings can make money only in productive age, exception is very rare due to biological limitations.

♣♣♣*(326)*♣♣♣
Money can change attitudes of people you never expected. Wealth generates envy. Money induces selfishness and irresistibly invites abuse .

♣♣♣*(327)*♣♣♣
Those who can afford today can only buy tomorrow. We are paying for our dreams. Money controls your time. Money buys you the freedom. When you are borrowing money beyond your capacity you are sabotaging your future.

♣♣♣*(328)*♣♣♣
Always think in terms of how to earn not how to spend. Disciplined will make money not smarter. Keeping money is a first step and investing wisely is second step to wealth creation.

♣♣♣*(329)*♣♣♣
Habit of expenditure remains whether you are rich or poor. Right place to store money is head not in heart. You need to

forgo few crucial years of expenditure of desires for having decades of financial freedom.

♣♣♣(330)♣♣♣

You can't control emotions and time. Just control your money it controls your everything. If you loose money, money starts controlling you.

♣♣♣(331)♣♣♣

Hack of modern life is money. Cool collects. Luck and risk are twins. Winning money is never a coincidental. Not earning but managing money is the real problem for wealth creation in the modern world due to too many distractions.

♣♣♣(332)♣♣♣

Ability to stick around long time makes difference for investment. Laziness is poverty. Income not spend is wealth. Desire less is a drive for wealth.

♣♣♣(333)♣♣♣

We all feel the world is too complicated and too difficult to like The fact it is never that complicated it is purely your perception. Your perception will be as you think. Hence how you are is more important for self understanding and perceiving your world.

♣♣♣(334)♣♣♣

Every human has own experiences in life. However, most carry forward these experiences to future by being pessimistic. Experiences are engraved in life due to emotions attached to it. Our brain processes these experiences based on lables thar we give to these experiences. Labels are meaning we give to our experiences. Hence be optimistic and label your life experiences in a constructive and positive way. How good is your present depends up on meaning that you give to your past experiences.

♣♣♣(335)♣♣♣

Non can born great. Your life depends upon how you develop as well as make use of you for the sake of self and others.

♣♣♣*(336)*♣♣♣

Remember being good need not be being moral and being moral need not be good. One has meaning of beneficial and other has meaning of being ethical.

♣♣♣*(337)*♣♣♣

You choose your personality with your attitude.

♣♣♣*(338)*♣♣♣

Your behavior is a result of your internal environment and external environment. Hence behavior changes with changed environment. Due to lack of courage to act as per our conscience our behavior succumbs to our environment . Our unhappiness has lot to do with our lack of courage to choose in our life.

♣♣♣*(339)*♣♣♣

Past never existed hence focus on present and future.

♣♣♣*(340)*♣♣♣

We can't live without people as we are social animals. Interpersonal relationships are essential to life. There is no ideal Interpersonal relationship. It is quite natural to get hurt in Interpersonal relationships hence you shouldn't take it to heart. You can't avoid Interpersonal relationships.

♣♣♣*(341)*♣♣♣

Most people lack courage to face reality. Boasting is reflection of a state of inferiority. Comparing with others makes us to feel inferior. We are humans, we are all equal despite our differences. But human to human is not same.

♣♣♣*(342)*♣♣♣

Competition feeling creates a perception enmity for others. Your state of mind will be good as long as you are only in competition with you.

♣♣♣*(343)*♣♣♣

When others are angry with you convey your intentions without anger cooly, but this needs some restraint.

♣♣♣(344)♣♣♣

However right nay be you, but you are not supposed to Criticize others. This is essential for maintaining Interpersonal relationships.

♣♣♣(345)♣♣♣

Threshold distance you need to maintain in Interpersonal relationships. Depending on your nature of relationships you need to maintain distance Interpersonal relationship. This is most important to maintain good relationships. Without this boundary limitation you can throw open to all. This gives enormous stress due to strained relationships.

♣♣♣(346)♣♣♣

All humans by default searches for faults and weaknesses in others. This negativity is more than five times powerful than positivity of seeing good in others. For having good perception of others needs some conscious rational effort.

♣♣♣(347)♣♣♣

One more disease that is affecting humans is judging others. Human automatically tries to judge others by default. When they stop judging others that will make their life happy and peaceful. Don't interfere with other life and tasks that will give you enormous disturbance in life.

♣♣♣(348)♣♣♣

To have fulfilled life you need self reflection to see whether you are living as per others expectations or as per your expectations.

♣♣♣(349)♣♣♣

Never crave for recognition or approval of others. Never be judged by others. When you want to please everyone by consensus you can't remain as good person rather you will be seen as a politician who promises everyone keeps non.

♣♣♣(350)♣♣♣

If other person do not like you it is their problem. You are not there to make everyone happy or please everyone, which is never possible. You live your life, not others life.

♣♣♣(351)♣♣♣
Never try to enforce your decisions on others rather help them
and assist them by making them aware of their situation that
enables them to take their own decisions or judgments.

♣♣♣(352)♣♣♣
Humans always wanted or crave to be liked by others in every
moment of life. Being disliked by others give stress to them.
Simple praise or appreciation makes them feel very good.
Hence always try to appreciate or praise others even in
negative situations that rejuvenate situations.

♣♣♣(353)♣♣♣
In the end all problems in personal life and professional life are
Interpersonal problems only.

♣♣♣(354)♣♣♣
Have gratitude by frequently using word THANK YOU.

♣♣♣(355)♣♣♣
Root cause for unhappiness is you want to be like others. When
you start to like yourself you will become a happy person.

♣♣♣(356)♣♣♣
Contribution to others and social work gives fulfillment and
satisfaction to individuals.

♣♣♣(357)♣♣♣
Your standards needs to be practical. If you keep high level
standards you can never achieve making everything messy.

♣♣♣(358)♣♣♣
Our body is designed to survive in threatened condition. Hence
all negative stimuli are processed on top most priority
(suppressing all other emotions and importance i.e. five times
more than positive stimuli. The threat can be emotional or
physical, body treats them as same. Even criticism rejection
and disliking are also taken as threat. They create enormous
distress. Threat can be real or imaginary, they are seen as
same. Hence state of mind and rational thinking are very
important for balanced positive mental state. It is individual
responsibility to distinguish real threats from imaginary threats.

Perception of threat triggers negativity in an unending loop or cycle. Unless it is terminated this chain reaction loop intensity will keep on building. Unless it is curtailed during initial phase, chain reaction forces permanent alterations in brain chemistry creating mental disorders. Imagination is God's blessing as well as curse to humans.

♣♣♣(359)♣♣♣

You can't remain happy without limiting and controlling your emotions. Your internal environment conditions plays major role than your external environment conditions for determining your happiness.

♣♣♣(360)♣♣♣

Ego is self created imaginary identity card of self. Ego is main cause of distressed Interpersonal relationships. Lack of self awareness creates ego. Craving of ego is infinite and can never be satisfied.

♣♣♣(361)♣♣♣

Our bad habit of comparison with others is created due to our ego. Comparison habit consequences are one of the main human sufferings of modern time.

♣♣♣(362)♣♣♣

More emphasis is given to record Negative emotions in our memory than positive emotions. Hence try not to get attached to negativity and learn to forgive and forget.

♣♣♣(363)♣♣♣

Your present state of mind is like a balance of a bank account with credits (positive emotions and debits (negative emotions . What you want to deposit in your bank account is only up to you. When debt (negativity unpaid for prolonged period it claims (your body.

♣♣♣(364)♣♣♣

Our mind loves comfort. This is the main reason for resistance to change. Some effort is required to push out of our comfort zone. Most of the times we suffer not because of lack of ability but due to lack of initiative. It is starting trouble.

♣♣♣(365)♣♣♣
Try to use positive and constructive affirming words for self and others. This will create reciprocal positive motivating influence around you.

♣♣♣(366)♣♣♣
When you are in negative environment either you ignore environment or quit environment or change environment.

♣♣♣(367)♣♣♣
Ear possess more soothing effect on state of mind than eye. Hence listen to music to relax.

♣♣♣(368)♣♣♣
Don't attach tags to people and things on your interaction, based on your temporary emotions. Everything is temporary and keeps on changing with time and circumstances. See things as they are rather as you feel.

♣♣♣(369)♣♣♣
Modern humans are suffering more from E-emotions due to social media. Restrict and restraint using social media.

♣♣♣(370)♣♣♣
Emotions can't be controlled but they have to be managed with logical and rational thinking of mind. You can't stop your emotions you have to compulsory experience the emotions and there is no other way.

♣♣♣(371)♣♣♣
Mind sets auto goal. Mind converts our imagination into reality. Hence imagine positive things with positive attitude. Mind generates positive emotions for your goal achievement.

♣♣♣(372)♣♣♣
Mind by default prevent you from doing exhausting and fearing things.

♣♣♣(373)♣♣♣
Never try to do too big things beyond your abilities and resources.
Break down big things in to small things and distribute among others for going. Integrate output of all.

♣♣♣(374)♣♣♣
Fear has many manifestations. Most of the fears are illusionary and melts away when faced.

♣♣♣(375)♣♣♣
Life changing events causes unbearable distress ones life. Trauma is created in life changing events. Seek help of your psychological counselor for managing its consequences.

♣♣♣(376)♣♣♣
Fatigue is creates chronic stress. Either share your task or seek help of others. Every time everything you can't do yourself. There has to be solution.

♣♣♣(377)♣♣♣
Act with thoughtfulness and purposefulness in life that gives no regrets in life.

♣♣♣(378)♣♣♣
Everyone will not treat you the way you like. Treating people is reciprocal, they way you treat others will come back to you.

♣♣♣(379)♣♣♣
Caffeine (tea, coffee and cold beverages has adverse affect on state of mind.

♣♣♣(380)♣♣♣
Loneliness is generator of stress as we are social animals. We can't live without others. When you can't reach others physically use other modes of communication like social media or electronic devices to be in touch with others. Other way you can engage your self by reading books or watching TV or movies. Join clubs or groups or communities or spiritual gatherings or start hobby or nourish pets or gardening.

♣♣♣(381)♣♣♣
Anything in excess doing is bad. Limit and   optimize in everything you do.

♣♣♣(382)♣♣♣
Spending some time in nature will distress you. Nature's smell, sounds, vision, touch, feeling has magical healing soothing affect on humans.

♣♣♣(383)♣♣♣

Before going to bed spend some time on bed reading books for removing distractive thinking about our that days activities.

♣♣♣(384)♣♣♣

Modern day news bulletins are more with negativity. Hence never start your day in morning with watching news bulletins. Morning time start with listening to good music.

♣♣♣(385)♣♣♣

Better time management resolves most of our problems causing distress.

♣♣♣(386)♣♣♣

For better task management you need to segregate your tasks into important and urgent tasks. Use schedules and schedulers. Set upper time limit for each task.

♣♣♣(387)♣♣♣

Adequate preparation supported by good planning prevents anxiety and stress.

♣♣♣(388)♣♣♣

Stress negatively affects directly or indirectly reproductive system.

♣♣♣(389)♣♣♣

Stress creates addictions such as alcohol, cigarettes or narcotics etc. These habits are natural human tendencies for managing stress. Stress also makes one to take very high risks which is dangerous to self and others.

♣♣♣(390)♣♣♣

Following scheduled routines in personal and professional life's will help in coping with stress preventing procrastination.

♣♣♣(391)♣♣♣

Stress created by health when you don't care self and your loved ones. You are the best doctor for self and your loved ones. Monitor self and your loved ones with health checking gadgets at home. Routinely get health checkup done and trend test reports. Major health problems can be averted from home by being vigilant.

♣♣♣(392)♣♣♣

Isolate your self from modern technology some times in a month and live in nature without any distractions.

♣♣♣(393)♣♣♣

Laugher is one of the easy ways to remove stress. Watch comedy show or movie or fun program or listen to jokes. Participate in fun games. Entertain and host a good friend.

♣♣♣(394)♣♣♣

Whatever the demands of your personal and professional lives self care is most important.

♣♣♣(395)♣♣♣

Stress is highly contagious. Unchecked stress spreads and affects others too. Stress breakdown our personality. Consequences of stress are enormous and far reaching. Stress makes day to day living difficult.

♣♣♣(396)♣♣♣

Unbalanced diet and unhealthy can cause stress. Mind and body must be nourished with balanced diet as per state of body internally and externally. Avoid processed food. Eat that much quantity which your body consumes and doesn't store as fat.

♣♣♣(397)♣♣♣

Familiarity, practice and creating a feeling of secure also reduces stress levels.

♣♣♣(398)♣♣♣

When you don't have self reflection you can't understand and manage your emotions.

♣♣♣(399)♣♣♣

Identify your bad habits causing stress slowly replace them with tiny good habits.

♣♣♣(400)♣♣♣

Avoid or shield your self from toxic people or situations.

♣♣♣(401)♣♣♣

Build network of people who support you, motivate you, help you, care you in life.

♣♣♣*(402)*♣♣♣
While Delegating in Interpersonal relationships trust them but verify periodically. Never give unchecked freedom to any one. Do regular follow-ups.

♣♣♣*(403)*♣♣♣
Use technology to make things simple, easy and productive. Unfamiliarity of technology causes stress.

♣♣♣*(404)*♣♣♣
Always have a team of your well wishers for advising.

♣♣♣*(405)*♣♣♣
Continuously educate your self and your people with changing circumstances and conditions. Use mentors.

♣♣♣*(406)*♣♣♣
Don't carry your mental baggage, history, desires, fears, opinions, judgments, pains, feelings. They are capable of over taking you.

♣♣♣*(407)*♣♣♣
Everyone is perfectly imperfect. Accept imperfections as a part of life. Mistakes are common, every one does.

♣♣♣*(408)*♣♣♣
Never be rigid in life by being non flexible. Be flexible in life with changing circumstances like a flowing water and move ahead. Life is a flow you can't stop it, you have to under go through it.

♣♣♣*(409)*♣♣♣
Put efforts to slowly shift your modern life style to natural life style.

♣♣♣*(410)*♣♣♣
Always have goals in personal and professional lifes. Goal makes things in order and prevents chaos and confusion. Goals and time will go hand in hand.

♣♣♣*(411)*♣♣♣
Stress is as low as you make your life simple.

♣♣♣(412)♣♣♣

When we are stressed, our subconscious mind is bypassed and we will lose our conscience of rational thinking, our heart takes control of us. We will become impulsive and reactive without thinking. Whenever you are emotionally disturbed, write down your feelings in a notebook in a language that you are most expressive. Our emotional disturbance is momentary. Whenever we write our feelings, what happens is our subconscious mind is automatically brought into action. Our subconscious mind tells to our heart how strange and odd our emotional feelings are. Life of our emotions is only for few seconds, after which they die down. By writing, you have delayed your reactive reaction, automatically, your feelings are nullified. When you read back your written feelings for few times, you will realize with your rational thinking how foolish and unnatural were your feelings.

♣♣♣(413)♣♣♣

Human life is nothing but experienced feelings. Our feelings are created with our emotional oscillations. We always experience emotions all the times, our existence itself is emotional, however only few emotions that are either pleasant or unpleasant are engraved in us as memory as experience. Stress is one such thing. Depending upon the severity or depth of our emotions, the experience of emotions is carried forward to the future, some for a short period of some forever. Extreme negative feeling in this we call it as trauma. Dairy writing is one of the beautiful ways of coping with stress. Never shy to express yourself, write down your every emotion and every experience of day. Read back your dairy daily, weekly, monthly. This gives self reflection of your personality and trains your subconscious mind. Your subconscious mind automatically unconsciously corrects your future personality and behavior from your earlier odd behavior. It creates an awareness of how untrue your emotions and feelings are.

♣♣♣*(414)*♣♣♣

Modern life is a dilemma between choices. In modern Era, everything is so much differentiated that we have too many choices to choose from. Our brain is primitive and not designed for modern age. Our brain can think only about one thing at a time, we can't simultaneously think about multiple things. Every stage of modern life we are presented with too many choices. The fundamental problem is decision-making and choosing of an alternative from multiple choices. Hence modern humans experience enormous stress while decision making due to their inability to evaluate all the alternatives due to their limitations. Switching over to simplicity and simple thinking will reduce their problem considerably.

♣♣♣*(415)*♣♣♣

Our excessive thinking converts small and negligible issues as big problems. Excessive thinking is self-defeating. Due to excessive thinking we start to feel all our thoughts are problems. Over thinking feeds to our negativity and fears.

♣♣♣*(416)*♣♣♣

Our emotional triggers and fluctuations are momentary in nature, if we delay our response by few minutes by engaging or diverting ourselfs to some other activity we can escape this emotional trap.

♣♣♣*(417)*♣♣♣

Environmental factors are more influential than internal factors creating anxiety and stress.

♣♣♣*(418)*♣♣♣

How do the stress affects individual depends upon his individual cognitive processing ability and his mental models of perception.

♣♣♣*(419)*♣♣♣

We are used to our environmental settings, when we encounter altogether different environments with new settings we will become stressful. Try to familiarize to new environment with repeated encounters.

♣♣♣(420)♣♣♣
When you feel stressful, find out what factor is causing the stress, if your interaction with that factor is not mandatory in your life, remove it from your life or else walk away from it. You shouldn't be affected when not required to be so.

♣♣♣(421)♣♣♣
Don't bottle up, express your self, communicate your feelings and needs.

♣♣♣(422)♣♣♣
When you have to be compulsorily in stressful situations try to modify your situation to the extent you can manage your stress.

♣♣♣(423)♣♣♣
When you can't manage your stress accept the situation. Acceptance does not mean your agreement. You are accepting the consequences of your situation. Acceptance gives learning from situation and resilience to start afresh with more energy. Acceptance relive you from stress.

♣♣♣(424)♣♣♣
There are situations in life you have to live with stress. Under such circumstances you need to use stress coping tools and techniques to manage adverse affects of stress.

♣♣♣(425)♣♣♣
When stressed calibrate your human senses. Focus on one human sense at a time at micro level try to feel it's sensations by simulating and try to enjoy it's feeling. Change over to other senses one after another i.e. vision, smell, touch, sound, taste etc. This breaks earlier panic of brain and makes you mindful and calm.

♣♣♣(426)♣♣♣
No human is exempt from having problems, everyone do have problems. Real problem is blaming self for having problems. Problem are not stationary they pass with time. Our suffering depends upon how do we respond to problems. We only have control over our response to the problem.

♣♣♣(427)♣♣♣

Indulging in an activity or hobby of creativity keeps your stress away. Do creative activities like painting, dance, singing, drawing, writing, sculpture etc

♣♣♣(428)♣♣♣

Try to improve connections with people those who illuminate your daily life with cheerfulness, joy and inspiration.

♣♣♣(429)♣♣♣

You will become stressful when you spend your energy and resources on least important things in your life. Your focus must be on your priorities.

♣♣♣(430)♣♣♣

How do you decide what is important in your life. Important things are things that enables and brings you towards closer to your short term or long term goals.

♣♣♣(431)♣♣♣

Urgent things are things that are time bound and penalties for not doing them proves to be costly.

♣♣♣(432)♣♣♣

You have to delegate activities that are unimportant but urgent to others.

♣♣♣(433)♣♣♣

Remove activities that are unimportant and not urgent from your daily to do list.

♣♣♣(434)♣♣♣

Life is limited, you can't plan for everything in life. Uncertainty and randomness is character of life.

♣♣♣(435)♣♣♣

Don't blame past. Seek new ways of thinking to resolve.

♣♣♣(436)♣♣♣

Your relationships must enable you to flourish and grow.

♣♣♣(437)♣♣♣

We can't get better without genuine love and authenticity in relations. They are essential to life.

♣♣♣(438)♣♣♣
To avoid trauma see history optimistically.
♣♣♣(439)♣♣♣
Life was designed simple, we humans tend to complicate it.
♣♣♣(440)♣♣♣
Celebrate your life or play it as entertainment.
♣♣♣(441)♣♣♣
Those who are students involved in formal learning, indulging in extracurricular activities, are helpful in reducing and eliminating stress levels.
♣♣♣(442)♣♣♣
There are many good things and bad things about social media. Social media disturbs one's concentration and focus. Prolonged exposure to social media alters one's natural thinking. When one encounters realities of life they feel disturbed as their social media altered perceptions do not match with that of ground realities.
♣♣♣(443)♣♣♣
Negativity is approximately five times more contagious and influential than positivity. Hence keep away from negative people those who are causing stress to you.
♣♣♣(444)♣♣♣
Create a like minded people's group on common grounds those who love you, care you, feel you, guide you, help you, improve you, spend time with you. They can be your friends, relatives, colleagues, or community groups.
♣♣♣(445)♣♣♣
List out all your postponed procrastinated activities with since date. Daily review the list out of which take up any important three activities that are causing stress to you due to postponement.
♣♣♣(446)♣♣♣
Swimming is one of the useful physical activities which had immediate affect to reduce stress.

♣♣♣*(447)*♣♣♣
Time to time attend inspirational seminars, events, lectures,
programs that impart positivity in life.

♣♣♣*(448)*♣♣♣
Create your own time.

♣♣♣*(449)*♣♣♣
However negative may be your environment, not losing your
positivity is key to reducing stress levels.

♣♣♣*(450)*♣♣♣
Building a reliable social network is important as ineffective
social support causes enormous stress.

♣♣♣*(451)*♣♣♣
Whatever you do, do if it has any logic, logic can be either
rational or non rational. If you do things that has logic,
subsequently, you don't regret.

♣♣♣*(452)*♣♣♣
Be what you are, never be conditioned by your environment or
else your conscience will curse you.

♣♣♣*(453)*♣♣♣
Your attachments, ego, judgmental, competition, comparison,
expectations, blaming attitudes are prime contributors of
stress.

♣♣♣*(454)*♣♣♣
Never mentally lable things, see as they are. Things are
subjected to change with time and circumstances.

♣♣♣*(455)*♣♣♣
Unbalanced romance and marriage life causes stress as
romance and marriage are important mile stones of life.

♣♣♣*(456)*♣♣♣
Periodic breaks of vacation are essential to life to live life of
stress free.

♣♣♣*(457)*♣♣♣
Logic is an asset to deal with stress.

♣♣♣*(458)*♣♣♣
Conditioned mind distorts realities, hence be natural.

♣♣♣(459)♣♣♣

Most disappointments come from expectations of conditioned mind, which is unreal.

♣♣♣(460)♣♣♣

Modern humans live in virtual unreal world of prejudices.

♣♣♣(461)♣♣♣

You are not born to live busy. Busy is an acquired habit.

♣♣♣(462)♣♣♣

When you deliberately confront with reality you will be stressed.

♣♣♣(463)♣♣♣

Information overload causes anxiety and stress as you can't filter out what is needed.

♣♣♣(464)♣♣♣

Plan and follow realistic schedules.

♣♣♣(465)♣♣♣

Wherever you are track your work and activities.

♣♣♣(466)♣♣♣

Break long-term goals into short-term goals. Create short-term deadlines and achieve them stress free.

♣♣♣(467)♣♣♣

Humans feel stress when their basic physical and emotional needs are not fulfilled.

♣♣♣(468)♣♣♣

Low level of stress is helpful and makes you more productive.

♣♣♣(469)♣♣♣

Stress due to modern technology is creation of modern Era.

♣♣♣(470)♣♣♣

Avoid unnecessary stress and manage necessary stress with tools.

♣♣♣(471)♣♣♣

Time is costlier than money.

♣♣♣(472)♣♣♣

Have realistic expectations. Limit your expectations.

♣♣♣(473)♣♣♣
Having body massage relaxes you.
♣♣♣(474)♣♣♣
Don't be doormat. Express you, individual you.
♣♣♣(475)♣♣♣
Double check important things.
♣♣♣(476)♣♣♣
Move with people who are better than you from whom you can learn.
♣♣♣(477)♣♣♣
Take a break from cell phone.
♣♣♣(478)♣♣♣
Good fragrance, stimulate your senses, and relax you.
♣♣♣(479)♣♣♣
Take responsibility for your own actions.
♣♣♣(480)♣♣♣
Focus on one thing at a time by being mindful.
♣♣♣(481)♣♣♣
Don't hide you NO. Don't say YES when you want to say NO.
♣♣♣(482)♣♣♣
Same way repeatedly doing by repetition can solve your problems because results will be same.
♣♣♣(483)♣♣♣
Never transmit your stress to others.
♣♣♣(484)♣♣♣
Keep your self busy such that you don't have time to feel stress.
♣♣♣(485)♣♣♣
When stress is inevitable, prepare a plan to cope consequences of stress.
♣♣♣(486)♣♣♣
When you feel difficulty in connecting with people in social gatherings, try to connect to individuals by asking about individuals' and families.
♣♣♣(487)♣♣♣
Learn from situations.

♣♣♣(488)♣♣♣

Keep trying, never give up.

♣♣♣(489)♣♣♣

Shield yourself from other people's stress affect.

♣♣♣(490)♣♣♣

Making educated decision is always better than indecision.

♣♣♣(491)♣♣♣

Be purposeful in what ever you do.

♣♣♣(492)♣♣♣

Prevent fatigue. You can't be everything to everyone.

♣♣♣(493)♣♣♣

Forget past regrets and focus on present now.

♣♣♣(494)♣♣♣

Hot water batch relaxes body.

♣♣♣(495)♣♣♣

Learn from others.

♣♣♣(496)♣♣♣

While discussing with others never point out individuals only point out subject point.

♣♣♣(497)♣♣♣

You are treated the way you allow others to treat.

♣♣♣(498)♣♣♣

Eliminate unhealthy food habits.

♣♣♣(499)♣♣♣

Big change causes stress. Gently accept it.

♣♣♣(500)♣♣♣

Complaining will boomerang.

♣♣♣(501)♣♣♣

Try to view situations from positive and constructive perspective.

♣♣♣

Acknowledgements

I am thankful to my family i.e. daughter Gummadi Pavani, mother Baby Samrajyam Gummadi and wife Swapna Gummadi with who's help I could author this book.

VIJAYKUMAR GUMMADI

♣♠♣

About Author

Mr VIJAYKUMAR GUMMADI is an Chemical Engineering & Business Management(MBA) Professional and a Nuclear Technology Specialist.

He is also an Certified International Project Management Expert with more than thirty five years of experience in eight industries of six states.

Developing Creative, innovative Business & Management Skills and Techniques and writing books are his Area of Self Interest.

He has Authored many Books that includes Best Selling International Paperbacks and e-Books.

For other Book details please visit last pages of this book.

♣♣♣

EASY MANAGING GUIDE FOR MODERN MANAGERS & EMPLOYEES

This book brings out 825 nos easy & immensely practical tips and sound advise under 75 managing aspects of organisation for helping modern managers and employees.

ISBN 9798885464321 (ENGLISH)
ISBN 9798889233923 (TELUGU)

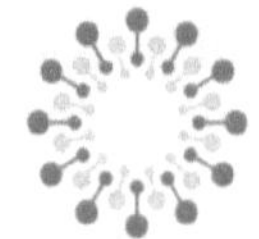

GOOD OFFICE TIPS

This book presents 710 nos useful tips for managing modern offices and organisations for implementing wonderful practices for improvement. These tips are based on modern time tested wisdom.

ISBN 9798890028129 (ENGLISH)
ISBN 9798890674487 (TELUGU)

Available at AMAZON and FLIPKART

www.ingramcontent.com/pod-product-compliance
Lightning Source LLC
Chambersburg PA
CBHW020752160726
47993CB00006B/2735